Bears

Kate Petty

BARRON'S

In the bears' den

Most bears live in cool places. They are among the biggest of the meat-eating mammals and need plenty of food to survive. Many of them sleep during the winter when food is scarce. A bear makes a den to sleep in, deep among the rocks, and lines it with leaves and moss. A mother bear mates in the spring or summer, but it is during her winter rest, safe and warm in her den, that she gives birth.

A pregnant Brown bear near her den

A Polar bear cub determined to wake its resting mom ▷

Newborn

There are usually two or three bear cubs in a litter. The cubs are minute compared with the size of their mother. Even the largest bears have cubs that are no more than 8 inches long and weigh less than 18 oz – about the size of a rat. Newborn cubs are pink and almost hairless, and utterly helpless. The mother bear washes the cubs all over. Her thick fur helps to keep them warm.

Three very young bears with their mother.

An Alaskan Brown bear nursing her cubs ▷

Early days

The new cubs spend most of their time asleep. They wake only to drink their mother's milk. The den is cozy compared with the wintry world outside. The mother doesn't go out but lives off the fat stored in her body. Her milk is rich and the cubs quickly put on weight. By the time they are three months old the cubs are ready to venture out of the den with their mother.

The cubs grow fat and round on milk from their mother.

A three-month-old Grizzly bear cub ▷

Learning with mother

When very young bear cubs first start to explore the world outside the den they are still completely dependent on their mother for food and protection. They follow her about wherever she goes. By watching their mother, the cubs learn how to find food. At first they catch ants and caterpillars, but soon they learn to catch mice and voles and other small animals to vary their mostly vegetarian diet.

Four-month-old cubs

The little bears stay close to their mother. ▷

Teeth and claws

A bear has sharp teeth for tearing at meat as well as flat teeth for grinding plants. Bears use their strong claws to overturn stones for insects, dig for roots or forage for fallen nuts and fruit. Claws are also useful for climbing trees. Bears climb in search of insects and seeds – and honey. Many kinds of bear love honey. They don't feel bee stings through their thick fur.

"Honey" bears (Malayan bears) in search of honey

This bear will learn to use its heavy paws and sharp claws for finding food. ▷

Bears in the water

Brown bears are good at fishing. As the weather gets warmer, the mother bear finds some shallow water for her cubs to splash about in. She teaches them to catch fish with their claws. When fish like salmon are plentiful, several bears gather together to catch them. Adult polar bears spend much of their time in the icy Arctic waters. Polar bear cubs don't learn to swim until their second year.

Playing in the water is a good way to cool off.

A bear takes its catch ashore to eat it. ▷

Bear senses

While her cubs are small the mother bear guards them fiercely against other hungry predators. But as they grow bigger and stronger, the bears have little to fear from other animals. Bears tend to eat whatever food is available – a bear is unlikely to chase after fast-moving prey. So a bear's most important sense is its sense of smell, which leads it to the food it needs to survive. A bear's sight and hearing are less keen.

American Black bear

Bears can stand up to get a better view. ▷

Preparing for winter

As their first summer draws to an end, the young bears are able to find most of their own food, although they still like to drink milk from their mother occasionally. At this time of year the bears need to eat all the food they can. The mother helps her cubs to find ripe fruit and nuts too, so they can feast before winter sets in. The family returns to the mother's den to sleep on and off through the winter.

Bears eating well before their winter sleep

16 At eight months the cubs can catch food for themselves but still they stay close to their mother. ▷

Leaving home

Most bear cubs stay with their mothers until well into their second year. Some stay until they are four years old. As they grow up, the cubs wander further and further away in search of food, and eventually they find territories of their own. From now on, they will probably live alone, meeting up with other bears only when food is plentiful or when it is time to mate.

This two-year-old bear is ready to take care of itself.

When her cubs have gone, the mother bear is ready to raise another family. ▷

Different bears

Different kinds of bears live in different parts of the world. The Polar bear, the huge white bear of the Arctic, has adapted to life in the snow and ice. Brown bears, sometimes called Grizzly bears, also live in cold places – Alaska, Canada and the USSR. The Sun bear lives in Southeast Asia. The Spectacled bear lives in South America. The Asian Black bear lives in the Himalayas and Southeast Asia.

Polar bear

Spectacled bear

Brown bear

Asian Black bear

Sun bear

The Sloth bear sucks up termites with a noise that can be heard 650 feet away. ▷

Bear facts

Although bears are the largest hunting mammals – a Kodiak bear can weigh nearly 880 lb and an adult European Brown bear weighs about 550 lb – they start life as one of the smallest, at less than 18 oz. Bears are intelligent animals that can be very dangerous when hungry or frightened or protecting their young. Most bears live in forests in the mountains, well away from human habitation.

Baby

Adult female

Adult male

Index

Photographic Credits:

Cover and page 17: Planet Earth Pictures; pages 3, 9, 13 and 15: Frank Lane Picture Agency Ltd; pages 5, 7, 19 and 21: Bruce Coleman Photo Library; page 11: Zefa.

Design	David West Children's Book Design
Illustrations	George Thompson
Picture Research	Emma Krikler

The publishers wish to thank Claire Robinson, Education Officer at London Zoo, for her assistance in the preparation of this book.

First paperback edition for the United States and Canada published 1992 by Barron's Educational Series, Inc.

First published in the United States 1991 by Gloucester Press.
© Copyright 1990 by Aladdin Books Ltd

All rights reserved.

All inquiries should be addressed to:
Barron's Educational Series, Inc.
250 Wireless Boulevard
Hauppauge, New York 11788

Library of Congress
Catalog Card No. 90-44447
International Standard
Book No. 0-8120-4964-0

Library of Congress Cataloging-in-Publication Data

Petty, Kate.
        Bears / Kate Petty.
        p. cm.--(Baby animals)
        Includes index.
        Summary: Color photographs and simple text describe the birth and development of a bear cub, its parents' care, and its social interaction.
        ISBN 0-8120-4964-0 (paperback)
1. Bears--infancy--Juvenile literature.
(1. Bears . 2. Animals--Infancy.) I. Title.
II. Series: Petty, Kate. Baby animals..
QL737.C27P43   1991
599.74"446--dc20   90-44447
                                            CIP   AC

Printed in Belgium
2345   987654321